Stuff

for Your

Space

Written by

Ellen Warwick

Illustrated by

Bernice Lum

Kids Can Press

To my grandmother, Vera — EW
for emma & charlotte — BL

Text © 2004 Ellen Warwick
Illustrations © 2004 Bernice Lum

KIDS CAN DO IT and the ☂ logo are trademarks of Kids Can Press Ltd.

Kids Can Press acknowledges the financial support of the Government of Ontario, through the Ontario Media Development Corporation's Ontario Book Initiative, and the Government of Canada, through the BPIDP, for our publishing activity.

Published in Canada by
Kids Can Press Ltd.
29 Birch Avenue
Toronto, ON M4V 1E2

Published in the U.S. by
Kids Can Press Ltd.
2250 Military Road
Tonawanda, NY 14150

www.kidscanpress.com

Edited by Stacey Roderick
Designed by Karen Powers
Photography by Frank Baldassarra

Printed in Hong Kong, China, by Wing King Tong

The hardcover edition of this book is smyth sewn casebound.

The paperback edition of this book is limp sewn with a drawn-on cover.

CM 04 0 9 8 7 6 5 4 3 2 1
CM PA 04 0 9 8 7 6 5 4 3 2 1

National Library of Canada Cataloguing in Publication Data

Warwick, Ellen
    Stuff for your space / Ellen Warwick ; illustrated by Bernice Lum.

(Kids can do it)

ISBN 1-55337-398-7 (bound).
ISBN 1-55337-399-5 (pbk.)

1. Handicraft — Juvenile literature.
2. Interior decoration — Juvenile literature. I. Lum, Bernice II. Title. III. Series.

TT160.W374 2004   j745.593   C2003-904254-5

Kids Can Press is a *Corus*™ Entertainment company

Contents

Introduction

Your space is the one place in the world that's all yours. So use it to show off your one-of-a-kind style, your stellar personality and your creative genius!

In this book you'll find fabulous ideas for making big or small changes, without spending lots of time or money. Whether you want to add a few hip accessories, spiff up an old look or just clear up the clutter, this book is for you.

Theme scheme

What is a theme anyway? A theme is an idea that inspires the way you decorate your space. It can be a hobby, such as basketball or piano. It can be a favorite symbol, such as stars or hearts. Or it can be a style, such as old-fashioned or trendy. The possibilities are endless. Choosing a theme for your room is an awesome way to make a statement about you and what makes you unique.

Need some help? Here are the themes that inspired projects in this book. Use these ideas to stimulate you, but don't be limited by them. You can adapt any project to your own special theme just by changing the colors or materials you use — be creative!

✦ Fun and Funky

Love to party all night long? Bright, jewel-tone colors and lots of sparkle and glitz make for a room with plenty of pizzazz.

✿ Think Pink

Are you proud to be a girly-girl? Surround yourself with anything and everything dainty and whimsical using flowers, ribbons, tulle and lots of pink and white.

⚽ Sporty Space

Hey, sports fan! Show off your love of athletics with this winning theme. Score extra points by using your team's colors and displaying trophies, equipment, team photos and souvenirs.

★ Starry Night

Want to feel like you're floating in the sky with stars, moons and clouds? Use silver or gold as a shimmering accent for colors such as dark blue, light blue or purple.

Color your world

Once you've chosen a theme, it's time to pick a color scheme. Choosing colors for your room and sticking to them when you're selecting the materials for the projects will pull the room's decor together.

And a well-chosen color scheme can affect the way you feel. Do you want a room that makes you calm and relaxed or one that makes you energized and lively? Use these tips and the color wheel to help you create the mood you want.

❁ *The cool colors (blue, green and purple) are quiet and soothing.*

❁ *The warm colors (red, yellow and orange) are exciting and energetic.*

❁ *Colors opposite each other on the wheel are complementary, which means they look dynamic together.*

❁ *Colors beside each other on the wheel are harmonious, which means they look calm together.*

Add white for a **tint,** a softer feeling color (for example, red becomes pink).

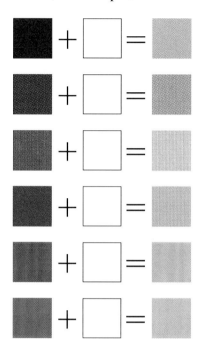

Add black for a **shade,** a deeper, more dramatic feeling color (for example, red becomes maroon).

Once you know what mood you want to create, choose your main color, or the color that is used most often.

Next, pick a second color, something either

complementary   or   **harmonious.**

If you have chosen complementary colors, a two-color scheme is perfect. If you have chosen harmonious colors, for example blue and purple, it's fun to choose a complementary third color, such as yellow. This third color can be used for small accents that will make your harmonious colors "pop," or stand out.

Things you'll need

You're almost ready to get crafting, but first here are some of the materials you'll need. Before buying any supplies, look around the house to see what you already have. Always ask permission before making any changes to your space or your stuff. Remember to protect your work surface and make sure an adult knows exactly what you'll be doing before you begin.

Glue

Any basic liquid white glue will do for many projects. A low-temperature glue gun also works well because it is easy to use and the glue dries quickly. Make sure you follow the directions on the glue gun package and have an adult standing by or helping when you use one.

Paint and paintbrushes

Acrylic craft paint is the best paint to use. It comes in lots of great colors and cleans up with soap and water. You can use any kind of paintbrush, but foam brushes coat most evenly. The size of the brush depends on the size of the area you're painting. For example, use a small brush to paint small details and a large one to cover a big area.

Spray paints and finishes

Acrylic spray paint leaves a nice even coat. Acrylic spray varnish is great for a clear, shiny finish. Always spray in a well-ventilated area, preferably outside, and cover your work area with newspaper or garbage bags. Remember to protect your clothing and to wear rubber gloves and a dust mask while spraying.

Utility knives

Always ask an adult to help you when using a utility knife. Protect the surface you are cutting on with a piece of corrugated cardboard, foam board or a cutting mat. For most projects, you can use scissors instead of a utility knife but the cut won't be as precise.

Fabric and trims

You can buy fabric, felt, fun fur and different trims, such as ribbon, tulle and marabou, from a fabric or craft supply store. Buy it by the meter (yard) or look for inexpensive ends and scraps. Old clothes can work, too. When working with fabric, be sure to use washable fabric glue and fabric paint.

Sewing tips

Most of the projects in this book use simple techniques, such as cutting, gluing and painting. For some projects, you'll need to know how to sew with a running stitch.

1. To begin, cut a piece of thread or embroidery thread about as long as your arm. Lick one end of the thread and carefully poke it through the needle's hole, or eye. Tie a knot in the other end of the thread.

2. Starting at the edge of your fabric, push the needle up through the fabric until the knot catches. Then, push it back through a little way over from the original hole. Gently pull the thread tight but not enough to make your fabric bunch up. Continue sewing, keeping your stitches the same size.

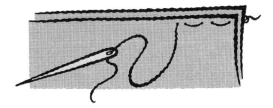

3. When you are finished sewing or are running out of thread, tie a knot close to the material and cut off the extra thread.

9

Groovy bead curtain

Get your room into the groove with this cool curtain.

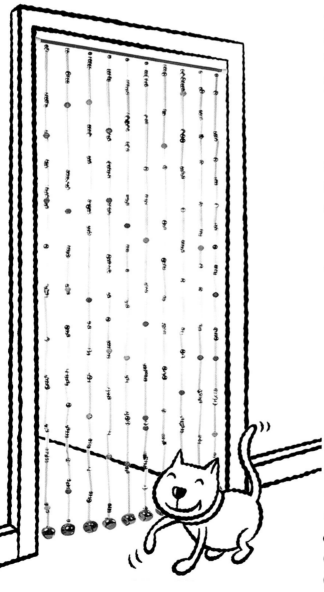

You will need

a curtain rod, the width of the inside of your door frame

acrylic spray paint

a box of colorful plastic drinking straws

string or twine, about 27 m (90 ft.)

10 large bells

plastic or glass beads, about 250

newspaper, rubber gloves, dust mask, a tape measure, scissors

1) In a well-ventilated area, spread out newspapers and lay the curtain rod on top. Wearing the gloves and mask, carefully spray paint the rod. Allow to dry and repeat.

2) Cut the drinking straws into long and short pieces.

3) Measure from the top to the bottom of the inside of your doorframe. Cut 10 pieces of string 15 cm (6 in.) longer than this measurement. (Or as many or few strands as you like — just be sure you have enough materials.)

4} Knot one large bell to the end of a string. Trim off any extra string.

5} Following a pattern or just deciding as you go, string the beads and straws onto the string until only 10 cm (4 in.) of string is left bare.

6} Repeat steps 1 to 5 to make the rest of the beaded strands.

7} Spacing them evenly, tie each beaded strand along the painted curtain rod. The large bell should be at the bottom of each string.

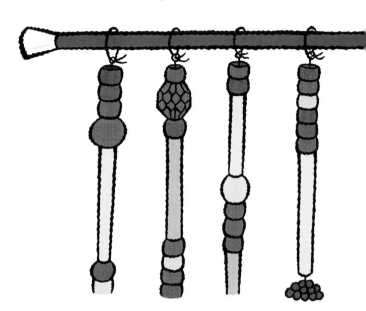

8} Ask an adult to help you install your groovy new bead curtain.

Other ideas

▦ Make a bead curtain for your window.

⚽ Get sporty and punch holes into the top and bottom of sports collector cards. String the cards between pieces of straw instead of beads in step 5.

11

Dangly doorknob bracelet

You won't have any surprise visitors with this jingly door adornment.

You will need

a 20 cm (8 in.) piece of thin elastic cord

20–30 large beads and buttons

six 50 cm (20 in.) pieces of ribbon

12 jingle bells

a ruler, scissors

1} Tie a knot 5 cm (2 in.) from one end of the elastic cord.

2} String the beads and buttons onto the other end of the cord. You can string them in a pattern or however you'd like. Continue stringing for about 10 cm (4 in.).

3} Knot the two cord ends together. Trim the ends.

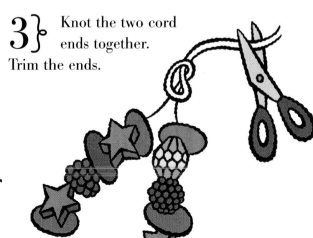

4} Spacing them evenly around the bracelet, tie the ribbons between the buttons and beads. The ribbon ends should hang down at different lengths.

5} Tie a jingle bell to each ribbon end. String a bead onto the ribbon first, if you like.

6} Place the finished doorknob bracelet around the doorknob on the inside or outside of your door.

Other ideas

Make one or two more bracelets to use as curtain tiebacks.

Make a smaller version for a ponytail holder.

13

Glitzy
jewelry box

Keep your most treasured trinkets in this glamorous box.

You will need

a plain wooden or cardboard box with a lid

gold acrylic paint

velvet or other soft fabric

plastic jewels

a medium paintbrush, newspaper,

a tape measure, scissors, a glue gun, white glue

1} Paint the outside of the box gold and let dry. Repeat.

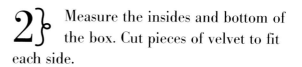

2} Measure the insides and bottom of the box. Cut pieces of velvet to fit each side.

3} Do the same for the lid.

14

4 Using the white glue, carefully glue on one piece of velvet at a time to the inside of the box and lid. Let dry before continuing.

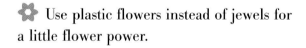

Other ideas

Instead of following steps 2 to 4, simply paint the inside of the box.

5 Use the glue gun to glue plastic jewels all over the outside of the box.

Use plastic flowers instead of jewels for a little flower power.

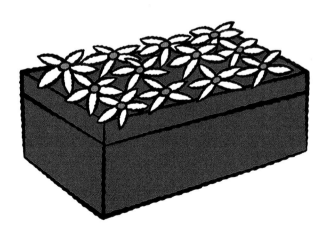

Fuzzy message board

Make a hard-to-miss spot for your messages.

You will need

a small framed chalkboard

acrylic paint

a small lidless plastic or cardboard box to hold chalk and an eraser

marabou

masking tape, newspaper, sandpaper, a damp cloth, a small paintbrush, a ruler, scissors, a glue gun

1} Carefully tape the chalkboard along the inside of the frame to protect the chalkboard while you paint.

2} Lightly sand the chalkboard frame to remove any shiny finish. Wipe it clean with a damp cloth.

3} Paint the chalkboard frame and the chalk holder. Let dry and repeat. Carefully remove the tape once the frame has dried.

4. Apply glue generously to one side of the small box and stick it to the bottom edge of the frame. Hold it in place until dry.

5. One side at a time, measure around the frame and chalk holder. Add these measurements together, then add 5 cm (2 in.) to this total. Cut a piece of marabou this length.

6. Use the glue gun to carefully apply glue to the edge of one side of the frame. Starting at one corner, press the marabou along the glued edge. Continue around the frame and chalk holder, gluing one side at a time. Trim off any excess marabou at the end.

7. Ask an adult to help you hang your new message board on your bedroom wall or door.

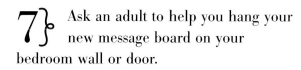

Other ideas

Make a matching chalk eraser by gluing marabou to its handle.

For a little star quality, paint the chalkboard frame midnight blue. Cut star and moon shapes out of tinfoil or other metallic paper and glue them around the frame.

Winning
wastebasket

*Blow the whistle on your mess
and give your garbage a time out.*

You will need

a large sheet of 5 mm ($^3/_{16}$ in.) thick black foam board

18 mm ($^{11}/_{16}$ in.) wide white electrical tape

four 115 cm (45 in.) red shoe laces

a metal-edged ruler, a pencil, a utility knife, a one-hole punch, scissors

1} In one corner of the foam board, measure and draw a rectangle 30 cm x 20 cm (12 in. x 8 in.), using the foam board edges for two of the sides. With an adult's help, use the utility knife and ruler to carefully cut out the rectangle.

2} Down the long sides of the rectangle, make a pencil mark every 2.5 cm (1 in.), 1 cm ($^1/_2$ in.) in from the edge. Hole punch a hole through each mark. (There should be eleven holes down each side.)

3} Using this first piece as a template, trace the shape and the holes onto the foam board three more times. Cut out and hole punch these three pieces.

4} For the white stripes, lightly draw lines every 18 mm ($1\frac{1}{16}$ in.) down the length of each piece of rectangle. One stripe at a time, cut a piece of electrical tape slightly longer than 30 cm (12 in.) and neatly lay it between the lines. Leave a stripe of black between each white stripe. Trim off any excess tape at the top and bottom of each foam board piece.

5} Starting at the bottom corner of two rectangles of foam, thread a shoelace through the first hole of each piece as shown. Pull the lace through the holes so it is an even length on both sides.

6} Continue to thread the lace through the holes, criss-crossing the two ends as you go. When you reach the top, tie a bow. Do the same with the other laces and foam rectangles to form a box shape.

7} Measure a 20 cm x 20 cm (8 in. x 8 in.) piece of foam board for the bottom. Cut it out with a utility knife.

8} Turn the wastebasket upside down and carefully push the base down inside to make a flat bottom. Use electrical tape along the edges to secure the base, making sure that the tape does not show on the sides of the wastebasket. Trim off any excess tape.

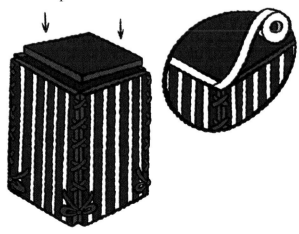

Note: This wastebasket is for dry waste only.

Baseball
clock

You'll always know when it's game time with this hit.

You will need

foam board, at least 5 mm ($^3/_{16}$ in.) thick

a battery-operated clock mechanism and battery

white, beige, red and blue craft foam sheets

a round dinner plate, a pencil, a utility knife, scissors, paper, white glue

1} For the clock face, lay the dinner plate on the white foam sheet. Trace around the plate. Remove the plate and cut the circle out with scissors. Next, cut a small hole in the center of the circle. This is for the clock mechanism to fit into.

2} Trace the foam circle from step 1 onto the foam board, including the center hole. With an adult's help, use the utility knife to cut the shape out. Neatly glue the circles together and let dry.

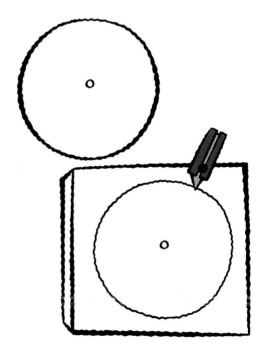

3} Following the package directions, attach the clock mechanism to the clock face.

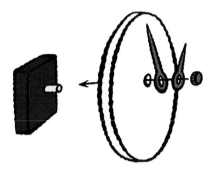

4} Trace the two baseball bats and the numbers from page 40 onto paper. Cut out the templates.

5} Trace the baseball bat templates onto the beige foam and carefully cut them out. Glue the long bat shape onto the long minute hand of the clock. Glue the short bat shape onto the short hour hand of the clock. Allow to dry.

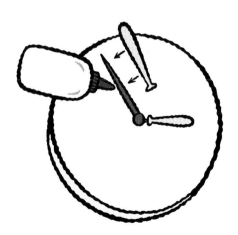

6} Trace the number templates onto the blue foam and carefully cut them out.

7} Glue the one and two (twelve) to the top of the clock face, six to the bottom, nine to the center left and three to the center right. Allow to dry.

8} Cut out twelve small red foam rectangles, 1.5 cm x 0.5 cm (⅝ in. x ¼ in.), to make the baseball stitches. Glue six stitches on each side of the clock face as shown.

9} Cut out a small blue foam circle and glue it over the base of the clock hands. Allow to dry.

10} Set the correct time and insert a battery into the back of the clock. Ask an adult to help you hang your new clock.

21

Tee-rific mirror

Score a hole in one with this mirror.

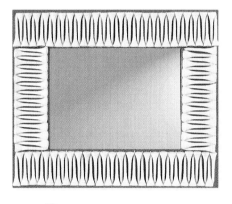

You will need

a mirror with a frame 5–10 cm (2–4 in.) wide

green acrylic paint

golf tees

masking tape, sandpaper, a damp cloth, newspaper, a medium paintbrush, white glue

1} Carefully tape the mirror along the inside edges of the frame to protect it while you work.

2} Gently sand the mirror frame and wipe it clean with the damp cloth.

3} Paint the frame with two coats of paint, letting each coat dry.

4 Apply a generous amount of glue along the top edge of the frame. Carefully glue the golf tees on one at a time, arranging the tees so that the pointed ends alternately face in and out. Repeat along the bottom edge.

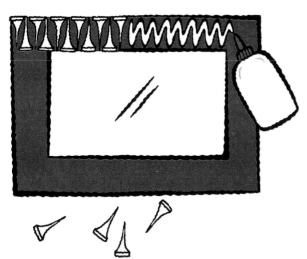

5 Glue the tees along the side edges of the frame, following the same in-out pattern. Let dry.

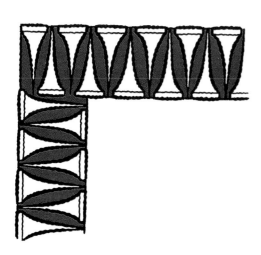

6 Ask an adult to help hang the mirror.

Other ideas

Make matching picture frames following the same steps on a plain wooden frame.

Create more theme-inspired frames and mirrors by gluing on small plastic toys, fancy buttons and other decorations.

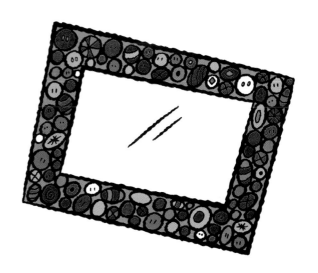

23

MVP
throw blanket

Show your team spirit with this cuddly blanket in your team colors.

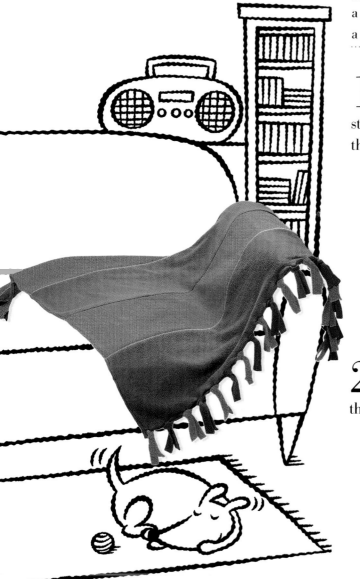

You will need

a 108 cm x 90 cm (43½ in. x 36 in.) piece of fleece in one color (A)

a 108 cm x 90 cm (43½ in. x 36 in.) piece of fleece in another color (B)

two 25 x 52.5 cm (10 in. x 21 in.) pieces of fleece, one in color A and one in color B

a tape measure, chalk, scissors, straight pins, a needle and thread

1} Measure and mark in chalk three 110 cm x 30 cm (43½ in. x 12 in.) strips on each large piece of fleece. Cut the strips.

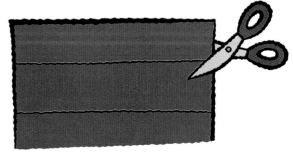

2} Lay the strips side by side, alternating the colors A and B. Pin the strips together as shown.

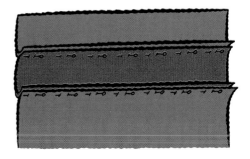

3} Sew along the pinned edges (see page 9), 2 cm (³⁄₄ in.) from the fabric edge. Remove the pins.

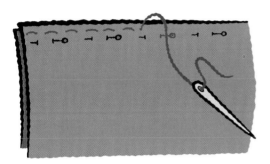

4} Lay the blanket out, wrong side up (sewn seams up). Pinning as you go, fold the edges over to make a 2 cm (³⁄₄ in.) hem.

5} Sew the hem and remove the pins.

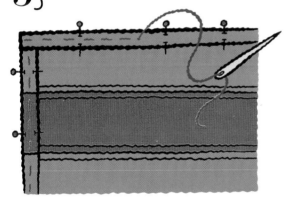

6} For the fringe, measure, mark and cut both small pieces of fleece into 25 cm x 2.5 cm (10 in. x 1 in.) strips. (You should end up with 40 pieces altogether.)

7} Using chalk, make small marks every 5 cm (2 in.) along the top and bottom of the blanket 2.5 cm (1 in.) from the blanket edge. With an adult's help, cut very small slits where you've marked.

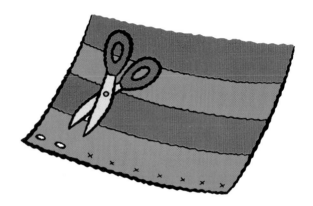

8} Fold a fringe piece in half. Poke the folded end up through a hole in the blanket and gently pull the loop through about 5 cm (2 in.). Push the free ends of the fringe piece through the loop. Pull the ends to tighten the knot. Continue adding the fringe pieces to the blanket, alternating the colors as you go.

25

Dazzling drawer knobs

Dress up your dresser or desk with these bead-encrusted knobs.

You will need

unfinished wooden drawer knobs
(to fit your drawers)

white air-hardening modeling clay

pink seed beads

acrylic sealer product such as Mod Podge

sandpaper, a damp cloth, a bowl filled with water, a plastic knife, a small plastic dish or container, a small paintbrush, newspaper

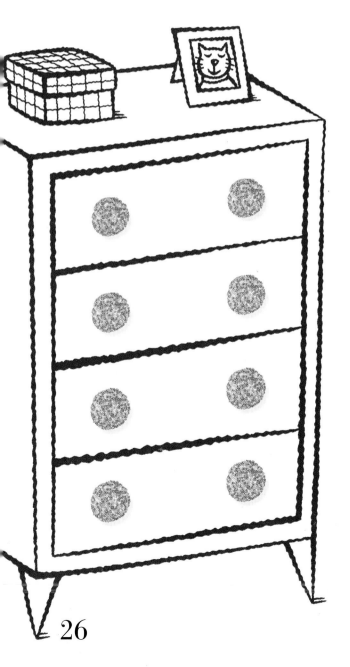

1} If you are using old knobs, sand them well to remove any shiny finish. Wipe them clean with a damp cloth.

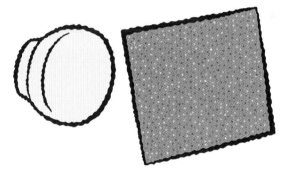

2} Working on one drawer knob at a time, soak each knob in water for a minute or so. This helps the clay to stick.

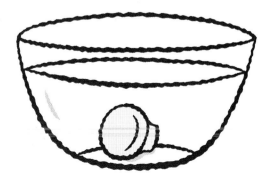

3} Knead a small piece of modeling clay in your hand until it is soft. Gently press the clay over the knob, smoothing it as you go. Dampen your fingers with water often to keep the clay workable and smooth. Continue working until you have an even 0.5 cm (¼ in.) layer of clay covering the knob.

5} Pour seed beads into the plastic dish. While the clay is still moist, roll the knob in the seed beads. Use your finger to gently press the beads into the clay, adding more wherever there is a bare spot. Once it is entirely covered with beads, set the knob beaded side up to dry overnight.

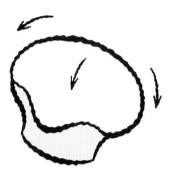

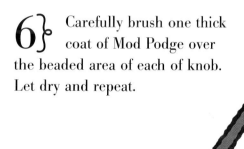

6} Carefully brush one thick coat of Mod Podge over the beaded area of each of knob. Let dry and repeat.

4} Use the plastic knife to trim any excess clay off the bottom of the knob. Make sure the bottom is completely clean.

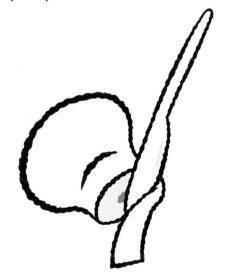

7} Once the second coat of Mod Podge has dried, ask an adult to help you put the beaded knobs on your drawers.

Tutu lamp shade

Your lamp will take center stage with its own ballet costume.

You will need

a plain white or beige lamp shade

pink acrylic paint

tulle

ribbon, 1.5 cm (⅝ in.) wide

ribbon rosettes, about 25

newspaper, a medium paintbrush,
a tape measure, chalk, scissors, double-sided
mounting tape, fabric glue, an elastic band

1} Paint the lamp shade with two coats of paint, letting each coat dry.

2} Wrap the tape measure around the bottom of the lamp shade and multiply this measurement by three. This is the width of tulle you'll need. For the length, measure from the top to the bottom of the lamp shade, add an extra 5 cm (2 in.) and multiply this number by two. Cut a piece of tulle to these measurements.

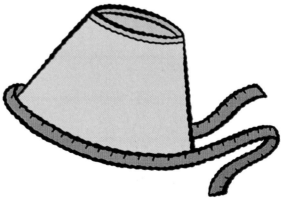

3} Fold the tulle in half lengthwise.

4) Stick double-sided mounting tape around the top of the lamp shade.

5) Starting at the back of the lamp shade, press the folded edge of the tulle firmly onto the tape, making even gathers as you go. Continue all the way around the lamp shade. Trim off any excess tulle.

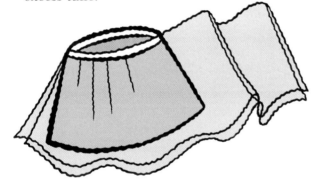

6) Measure around the top edge of the lamp shade and add an extra 2.5 cm (1 in.). Cut the ribbon to this length.

7) Spread fabric glue generously on the ribbon. Starting at the back of the lamp shade, press the ribbon around the top edge, covering the gathers of tulle. Use an elastic band to hold the ribbon in place while it is drying. (If the ribbon doesn't look smooth when it dries, cut another ribbon and carefully glue it over top.)

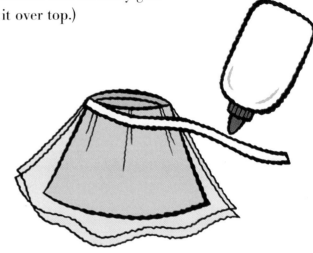

8) One at a time, apply fabric glue to the ribbon rosettes and glue them onto the tulle in a scattered pattern. Let dry before putting the lamp shade on the lamp.

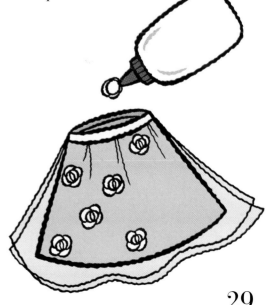

Sweet dreams pillowcase

Sleep well with this dreamy pillowcase.

You will need

felt in various shades of pink

5 small pink pompoms

5 small snaps

a pillowcase and matching thread

four 30 cm x 1 cm (12 in. x ½ in.) pieces of ribbon

a pencil, paper, scissors, chalk, straight pins, a needle

1} Trace the flower shape from page 40 onto the paper. Carefully cut it out. This is your template.

2} Use the chalk to trace a total of ten flower shapes onto the different colors of felt. Cut them out.

3} Place one color flower shape on top of another color flower shape as shown and pin them together. Sew them together, making the stitches in the middle of the flowers. Remove the pins.

4} Sew a pompom to the flower center, over the stitches you made in step 3. Turn the flower over and sew the snap backing in the middle.

5} Repeat steps 3 and 4 to make four more flowers in a variety of color combinations.

6} With chalk make five small evenly spaced marks along the pillowcase edge. This is where the felt flowers will be attached. Sew the five snap fronts on these marks. Snap the flowers in place.

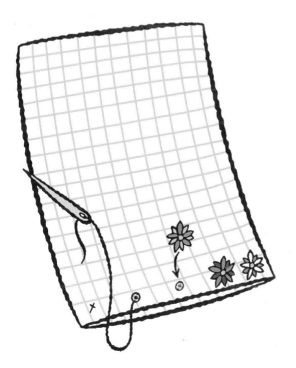

7} Turn the pillowcase inside out and lay it flat. Along one side of the open edge of the pillowcase, pin a ribbon 15 cm (6 in.) from each corner, as shown. Be careful not to pin the pillowcase together. Turn the pillowcase over and repeat.

8} Sew ribbon pieces in place using the needle and matching thread. Remove the pins.

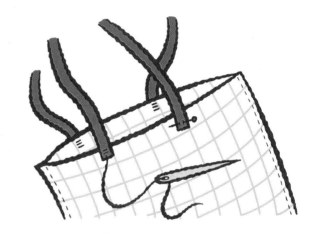

9} Turn the pillowcase right side out and put your pillow inside. Tie the ribbons into bows.

Note: Before washing the pillowcase, unsnap and remove the felt flowers.

31

Pretty in pink corkboard

Tuck special photos and mementos under lovely ribbons and fancy pushpins.

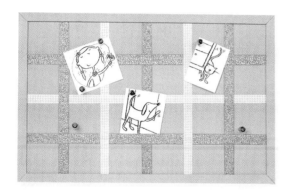

You will need

a corkboard with a removable wooden frame

pink acrylic paint

ribbon, 2 cm (¾ in.) wide

clear plastic pushpins

sequins

sandpaper, a damp cloth, a small paintbrush, a tape measure, a pencil, scissors, a glue gun, white glue

1} Carefully remove the frame from the corkboard. Lightly sand the frame and wipe it clean with a damp cloth.

2} Paint the corkboard, let dry and repeat. Do the same for the frame.

3} Measure the width of the corkboard and add 10 cm (4 in.). Cut three pieces of ribbon to this length. Lay the ribbons widthways across the corkboard so 5 cm (2 in.) hangs over each end. Working with one ribbon piece at a time, pull the ribbon tight and hold it in place with a few pushpins.

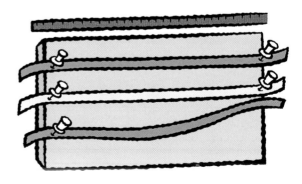

32

4} Measure the height of the corkboard and add 10 cm (4 in.). Cut five pieces of ribbon to this length. Weave them through the three pinned ribbons as shown so 5 cm (2 in.) hangs over each end. Pin the ribbons in place like you did in step 3.

5} Carefully turn the corkboard over. Working with one ribbon at a time, use the glue gun to put a dab of glue at each ribbon end. Pull each end tight and press it against the back of the board while the glue dries. Turn the corkboard over and remove the pushpins.

6} Put the frame back on the corkboard, and ask an adult to help you hang it.

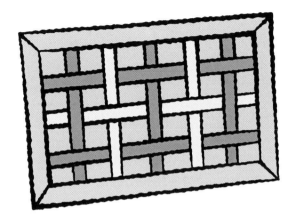

7} For the fancy pushpins, dab white glue onto the head of each pin, apply a sequin and let dry. Make about 15 or 20 for pinning up your special stuff.

Other ideas

★ Choose a piece of fabric to suit your theme or to match your color scheme. Remove the frame from the corkboard and stretch the fabric tightly over the corkboard. Glue the fabric edges to the back of the board and put the frame back on.

Lucky star pajama keeper

Tuck your pjs away in this enchanting pajama keeper.

You will need

a 33 cm x 70 cm (13 in. x 28 in.) rectangle of fabric

a small piece of non-fraying fabric for the star shape

embroidery thread

a tape measure, straight pins, a needle and thread, a pencil, a piece of paper, scissors

1. Fold a short edge of the fabric rectangle over 1 cm (½ in.). Fold it over again and pin in place. Repeat with other short edge. Sew along each folded side (see page 9). Remove the pins.

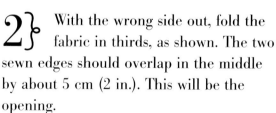

2. With the wrong side out, fold the fabric in thirds, as shown. The two sewn edges should overlap in the middle by about 5 cm (2 in.). This will be the opening.

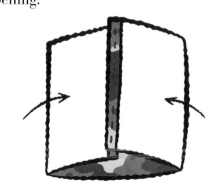

3} Pin and then sew along both open sides. Remove the pins and turn the pj keeper right side out.

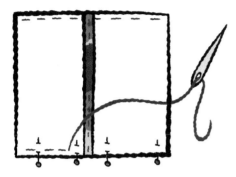

4} Trace the star shape from page 40 onto the paper and cut it out. Trace this star pattern onto the wrong side of the non-fraying fabric and cut it out.

5} Using the embroidery thread, sew the star onto the pj keeper. Be sure to sew through only the top layer of the fabric.

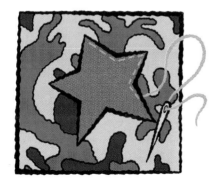

6} Slip your pjs in through the back opening and tuck the keeper under your pillow.

Other ideas

★ Make a smaller keeper with the same fabric to hide your diary.

Starry night
switch plate

The stars will shine, day and night, with this fancy switch plate.

You will need

a plastic switch plate and screws

dark blue acrylic craft paint

gold glitter, gold star stickers

acrylic spray varnish

sandpaper, a damp cloth, newspaper, a small paintbrush, masking tape, white glue, a cardboard box, rubber gloves, dust mask,

1} Lightly sand the plastic switch plate until it is no longer shiny. Wipe it clean with a damp cloth.

2} Paint the switch plate and screws with two coats of paint. Let dry.

3} Tape a band of masking tape above and below the switch opening.

4. Coat the switch plate with a layer of white glue. Generously sprinkle glitter over the wet glue. Let dry and gently shake off any loose glitter.

5. Carefully remove the masking tape. Apply star stickers to the areas where the masking tape prevented the glitter from sticking.

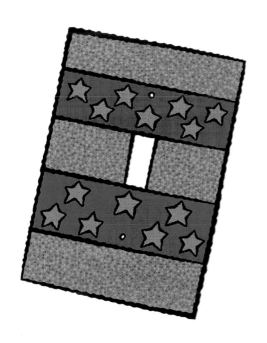

6. Place the switch plate in an open cardboard box. In a well-ventilated area, spray the switch plate with acrylic spray varnish. Let dry and repeat two more times.

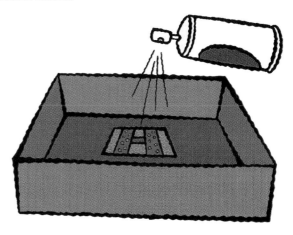

7. Ask an adult to help you install your new switch plate.

Other ideas

For a funky version, lightly sand a switch plate, and coat it with a thick layer of white glue. Press colorful plastic jewels and sequins into the glue to cover the entire surface, leaving the switch and screw holes uncovered.
Let dry.

Stellar area rug

Wiggle your toes on this fuzzy star.

You will need

a 90 cm x 90 cm (36 in. x 36 in.) square of yellow fun fur

a 110 cm x 110 cm (44 in. x 44 in.) square of blue fun fur

newspaper, tape, a long ruler or meter stick, a pencil, scissors, straight pins, a marker

1} Tape four sheets of newspaper together to make a 90 cm x 90 cm (36 in. x 36 in.) square.

2} Measure across the top of the newspaper and make a mark at 45 cm (18 in.). This is point A. Measure across the bottom of the newspaper and make a mark 15 cm (6 in.) in from each bottom corner. These are points B and C. Measure down 30 cm (12 in.) from each top corner and make a mark. These are points D and E.

3} Drawing straight lines, join the points together in the following order: A and B, A and C, C and D, B and E, D and E. You should have drawn a star.

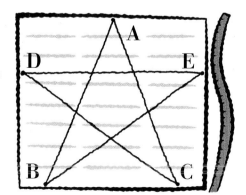

38

4} Cut around the star shape. This is your template.

5} Lay the yellow fun fur square right side (fur side) down, and place the template on top. Pin the template in place.

6} Using the marker, trace around the template and then unpin it. Carefully cut out the star you drew on the back of the fun fur.

7} Fold the blue fun fur square in half once and then again to make a smaller square. Along the corner that is not folded, round off all four layers. Be sure to cut evenly, one layer at a time.

8} Open the fun fur and lay it right side up. Place the fun fur star right side up in the center of the blue fun fur piece. Pin it in place.

9} Working on one star point at a time, remove the pins and fold the point toward the center of the star. Apply a line of glue along both edges of the star point and then press it back down in place. Let dry. Repeat for the other four points of the star. Let dry.

Other ideas

✿ Use another simple shape as a template to make an area rug that suits your theme, such as a heart, an initial or a team logo.

Templates

Number templates
(page 21)

Star template *(page 35)*

Flower template
(page 30)

Baseball bat templates
(page 21)